A Special Gift

For:

_____

From:

_____

Date:

_____

A Little Nest of Pleasant Thoughts

Brownlow

Brownlow Publishing Company, Inc.

LITTLE TREASURES
MINIATURE BOOKS

A Child's Tea Party · A Little Cup of Tea

A Little Nest of Pleasant Thoughts

All Things Great & Small

All Things Grow With Love

Angels of Friendship

Baby's First Little Bible

Baby's First Little Book

Baby's First Little Book of Angels

Dear Teacher · Faith
Faithful Friends · Flowers of Graduation
For My Secret Pal · From Friend to Friend
Grandmothers Are for Loving
Mother – The Heart of the Home
My Sister, My Friend
Precious Are the Promises
Quilted Hearts · Rose Petals
Soft As the Voice of an Angel
The Night the Angels Sang
'Tis Christmas Once Again

THE DAFFODIL FIELD

Went to the Daffodil field again.
The buds are just breaking into yellow.
Found two Thrush's nests, both in holly bushes;
one nest was empty, the bird was sitting on the
other; she looked at me with such brave, bright
eyes, I could not disturb her, much as I would
have liked a peep at her speckled blue eggs.

EDITH HOLDEN

There are two worlds: the world that
we can measure with line and rule,
and the world that we feel with our
hearts and imagination.

LEIGH HUNT

To be able to look back upon one's
past life with satisfaction is to live twice.

MARTIAL

Very little is needed to make a happy life.

MARCUS AURELIUS

The face is the mirror of the mind;
and eyes, without speaking,
confess the secrets of the heart.

ST. JEROME

CHEERFUL HEARTS

A cheerful look brings joy
to the heart, and good news
gives health to the bones. . . .
A cheerful heart is good medicine,
but a crushed spirit dries up the bones.

PROVERBS 15:30; 17:22

May you be as happy as a nest of singing birds.

We do not know how cheap the seeds of
Happiness are, or we should scatter them oftener.

JAMES RUSSELL LOWELL

It is in the enjoyment and not in mere possession
that makes for happiness.

MICHEL DE MONTAIGNE

LISTEN TO THE MOCKINGBIRD

I sincerely congratulate you on the arrival
of the mockingbird. Learn all the children to
venerate it as a superior being in the form of a bird,
or as a being which will haunt them if any harm is
done to itself or its eggs.

THOMAS JEFFERSON

There will be peace in the world so far as
there is righteousness in the heart.

JOHN MILLER

The trees of the Lord
are well watered,
the cedars of Lebanon
that he planted.
There the birds
make their nests.

PSALM 104:16, 17

We blossom under praise like flowers in sun
and dew; we open, we reach, we grow.

GERHARD E. FROST

I can never close my lips where
I have opened my heart.

CHARLES DICKENS

Existence is a strange bargain. Life owes us little;
we owe it everything. The only true happiness
comes from squandering ourselves for a purpose.

JOHN MASON BROWN

FRIENDSHIP & MEMORIES

Be happy; let who will be sad,

There are so many pleasant things,

So many things to make us glad,

The flower that buds, the bird that sings;

And sweeter still than all of these

Are friendship and old memories.

M.C.D.

SING THY PART

Wake for shame, my sluggish heart,
Wake, and gladly sing thy part;
Learn of birds, and springs, and flowers,
How to use thy noble powers.

JOHN AUSTIN

RICH THOUGHTS

It is only a poor sort of Happiness that
could ever come by caring very much about
our own narrow pleasures. We can only have
the highest Happiness by having
rich thoughts and much feeling for the
rest of the world as well as ourselves.

GEORGE ELIOT

Love builds the strongest nest.

ANONYMOUS

Is it so small a thing to have enjoyed the sun,
to have lived life in the spring, to have loved,
to have thought, to have done?

MATTHEW ARNOLD

Now and then it's good to pause in our
pursuit of happiness and just be happy.

ANONYMOUS

What the heart has once owned and had,
it shall never lose.

HENRY WARD BEECHER

Even the sparrow has found a home,
and the swallow a nest for herself, where she
may have her young a place near your altar,
O Lord Almighty, my King and my God.

PSALM 84:3, 4

If my heart is right with God,
every human being is my neighbor.

OSWALD CHAMBERS

A small house will hold as much
happiness as a big one.

ANONYMOUS

A Hidden Nest

It is a fascinating pursuit, when there is leisure for it,

to look for the nests in the garden or

neighbourhood of a country home.

The discovery of a well-hidden nest with eggs

gives a sense of delicate privilege; the watching

of its subsequent welfare is a continuing interest;

and if the end is happy and the young birds

leave the nest safely, we feel deeply satisfied.

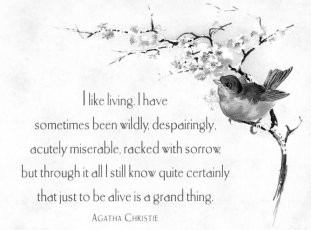

I like living. I have
sometimes been wildly, despairingly,
acutely miserable, racked with sorrow,
but through it all I still know quite certainly
that just to be alive is a grand thing.

AGATHA CHRISTIE

Life is made up, not of great sacrifices or duties, but
of little things, in which smiles and kindnesses and
small obligations win and preserve the heart.

HUMPHREY DAVY

LITTLE NESTS

Birds in their little nests agree;
And 'tis a shameful sight,
When children of one family
Fall out, and chide, and fight.

ISAAC WATTS

The foxes have holes, and the birds
of the air have nests; but the Son of man
hath not where to lay his head.

MATTHEW 8:20

Try to be happy in this present moment,
and put not off being so to a time to come,
as though that time should be of another make
from this which has already come, and is sure.

THOMAS FULLER

Be glad of life because it gives you
the chance to love and to work and
to play and to look at the stars.

HENRY VAN DYKE

There are no birds this year in last year's nest.

ITALIAN PROVERB

We Have Wings

Be like the bird

That, pausing in her flight,

Awhile on boughs too slight,

Feels them give way

Beneath her and yet sings,

Knowing that she

hath wings.

VICTOR HUGO

If wrinkles must be written upon our brows,

let them not be written upon the heart.

The spirit should not grow old.

JAMES A. GARFIELD

There's never a rose in all the world

But makes some green spray sweeter;

There's never a wind in all the sky

But makes some bird wing fleeter.

ANONYMOUS

Blessed are they who are pleasant to live with.

ANONYMOUS

THE HAPPY HEART

The happiest heart that ever beat

Was in some quiet breast

That found the common daylight sweet,

And left to Heaven the rest.

JOHN VANCE CHENEY

The Sunshine of Happiness

Happiness is the most accommodating of all things. It will come to a cottage as soon as to a palace. You need never wait for any outward pomp to come. As the sunshine of the Almighty will shine through a simple vine as richly as upon the velvet of a king or upon the gilded dome of a temple, so happiness falls with equal sweetness upon all whose minds are at peace and in whose hearts flow the good thoughts and good sentiments of life.

David Swing

Rejoice that your names are written in heaven.

LUKE 10:20

Make a nest of pleasant thoughts.

JOHN RUSKIN

Each of us is bound to make the little circle
in which he lives, better and happier.

A. P. STANLEY

Whoever is happy will make others happy too.

ANNE FRANK

A WREN'S NEST

The most remarkable instance of prolific
nest building is that of the common wren.
After the long-tailed tit's nest, that of the wren
is the most elaborate. Yet one pair of wrens
will make several nests; each nest is constructed
with great care and perfect skill; but only the one
that is destined for eggs is lined with feathers.

VISCOUNT GREY

One makes his own happiness only by
taking care of the happiness of others.

SAINT-PIERRE

There's a big difference between
putting your nose in other
people's business and putting your
heart in other people's problems.

ANONYMOUS

Happiness is neither within us,
nor without us; it is the union
of ourselves with God.

BLAISE PASCAL

PURE HEARTS

Give us a pure heart that we may see Thee;

A humble heart that we may hear Thee;

A heart of love that we may serve Thee;

A heart of faith that we may live Thee.

DAG HAMMARSKJÖLD

You will seek me and find me

when you seek me with all your heart.

I will be found by you.

JEREMIAH 29:13, 14

Hope is the thing with feathers

That perches in the soul,

And sings the tune without the words,

And never stops at all.

EMILY DICKINSON

While we are fascinated by birds to see their color,

to hear their music, to discover a hidden nest

with eggs, it is their mastery of flight that

provides their strongest appeal.

THE GIFT OF HAPPINESS

Do whatever comes your way to do as well as you can. Think as little as possible about yourself and as much as possible about other people and about things that are interesting. Put a good deal of thought into happiness that you are able to give.

ELEANOR ROOSEVELT

The art of being happy is the art of discovering the depths that lie in the common daily things.

BRIERLEY

Lord, send me where thou wilt, only go with me;
lay on me what thou wilt, only sustain me.
Cut any cord but the one that binds me
to thy cause, to thy heart.

Titus Coan

A real friend is one who will tell you
of your faults and follies in prosperity,
and assist you with her hand and heart
in adversity.

The Greatness of God

As the marsh hen secretly builds
on the watery sod,
Behold I will build me a nest
on the greatness of God.

Sidney Lanier

When you rise in the morning, form
a resolution to make the day a happy one
for a fellow creature. It is easily done.

Sydney Smith

If you cannot find happiness along the way,
you cannot find it at the end of the road.

ANONYMOUS

Life begets life. Energy creates energy.
It is by spending oneself that one becomes rich.

SARAH BERNHARDT

Delight yourself in the Lord
and he will give you
the desires of your heart.

PSALM 37:4

No bird soars too high,
if he soars with his own wings.

WILLIAM BLAKE

A kind heart is a fountain of gladness,
making everything in its vicinity freshen into smiles.

WASHINGTON IRVING

There is a big difference between living
and just breathing. Choose to live, not just exist.
Use your gifts and your days wisely, deliberately.
You were put here for a purpose.

PAUL C. BROWNLOW

BLESS THE BEASTS & SINGING BIRDS

Dear Father, hear and bless
Thy beasts and singing birds:
And guard with tenderness
Small things that have no words.

ANONYMOUS

Sing As the Thrushes Do

The young lambs are bleating in the meadows,

The young birds are chirping in the nest,

The young fawns are playing with the shadows,

The young flowers are blowing toward the west.

Go out, children, from the mine and from the city;

Sing out, children, as the little thrushes do;

Pluck your handfuls of the meadow-cowslips pretty,

Laugh aloud to feel your fingers let them through.

Elizabeth Barrett Browning

ILLUSTRATION CREDITS